DAWN OF A NEW DAY

A 21-Day Inspirational Journal to
Renew Your Faith, Mind & Spirit

Tiffaney Dale

TIFFANEY DALE AGENCY
DALLAS • HOUSTON

DAWN OF A NEW DAY

Published by Tiffaney Dale Agency

2201 Main Street, Suite 785

Dallas, Texas 75201

www.tiffaneydale.com

Copyright ©2016 by Tiffaney Dale

All rights reserved. No part of this publication may be reproduced or transmitted for commercial purposes, except for brief quotations in printed reviews, without written consent from the publisher. All scripture quotations are taken from the New King James Version of the Bible.

ISBN 978-0-9980871-0-8

Cover design by Demarcus McGaughey

Cover back photo by Cody Bess

Editorial Team: Elaine Garcia of Before You Publish and Michelle Chester of EBM Professional Services. Layout by Nakia Laushaul of A Reader's Perspective.

Library of Congress Control Number: 2016914579

Printed in the United States of America

DAWN OF A NEW DAY is lovingly dedicated to the memory and legacy of my beautiful mother, Dawn Jean Hunter Newton. Mother was the epitome of joy, strength, courage, and faith who never let the many obstacles in life deter her from fulfilling her dreams as well as God's purpose for her life. She was a funny, giving, caring, and natural beauty with a radiant smile and gracious heart that touched the lives of many. Her presence, laughter, and wittiness are loved and missed dearly.

This spiritual journal also celebrates the loving memory of my Granny, Lola Jean Hunter Garner, who's unconditional love, support, and wisdom served as the strong foundation for our entire family. Her warm heart and loving spirit continues to live on through the many lives that she raised, loved, touched, and blessed.

Acknowledgements

To my father, John C. Newton, my siblings: Ty-Ron, Whitney, and Johnathan, and my handsome nephew, Ty. I would also like to thank my amazing Hunter and Newton family, extended Kingsville family, host of friends, and the many Angels that have been placed along my path throughout my life's unique journey.

PREFACE

I, like most people, struggle on a daily basis to live a righteous life that is on a straight and narrow path. Often, I start off with the best of intentions, but somehow end up being right back to where I started—an emotional mess overcome with heavy feelings of frustration, confusion, guilt, and regret. Fed up with facing depressing days and sleepless nights haunted by consequences of poor decisions, I began to seek something deeper and more meaningful. A yearning that marked the beginning of my spiritual journey.

My first step was becoming a member of a church that I had been visiting for a while and joining its small women's fellowship group. This was a big deal for me because it was the first time that I began to tear down years of built up walls to share some of my emotional and spiritual obstacles with others. I enjoyed this new spiritual accountability and freedom; however, I made a beginner's mistake of seeking guidance and approval from those around me, rather than seeking that guidance and validation from within. Running around attempting to live up to human expectations, I found myself being more confused as I continued to encounter emotional and spiritual pitfalls. No matter how hard I tried to do the right thing, I somehow would get drawn back into the many distractions of the world.

My spirit was so torn as I lived through several months of confusion, conflict, and emotional emptiness—a period that I today reference as the "fog." Everything was unclear and I was simply going through the motions of life and in desperate need of a spiritual intervention. It was at this low point, while I was extremely thirsty for God's Word and guidance, that I made the effort to build my relationship with Him. For me, I knew the first thing I needed to do was spend some time alone and retreat from personal distractions like dating and being around toxic people. The emotional rollercoasters had worn me down and I just needed to be left alone to hear from Him.

Ironically, a few months prior I was given a spiritual journal as a gift from one of my "distractions." At the time I received the journal, I had tossed it to the side and had not even opened it long enough to see that there was a special message written for me in the front pages. However, on that particular day in July 2007, I opened it and began to experience an intimate relationship with my Heavenly Father.

Throughout the next few weeks, I rose early each morning, microwaved a bowl of instant oatmeal or prepared frosted flakes with fruit, and headed out onto the patio for breakfast and time with God. I would begin by reading a passage from the journal, followed by spending time reflecting on the message I had received. After letting the words seep into my soul, I would then spend a few minutes capturing my thoughts in the journal, which included my personal reflections, praises, and prayer requests. Once complete, I would head back inside and kneel in front of the sofa for intimate time in prayer. I would stay in prayer position until I received direction from Him through a deep knowing from within.

Honestly, my initial plan was to do this morning routine for only two weeks. So needless to say I was surprised when I looked up and several months had quickly come and gone. I never dreamed that this 30-minute morning ritual would become a daily routine that would truly transform my entire life. From personal relationships to professional endeavors, everything simply flourished.

Once I welcomed and received Him, every aspect of my life fell into place. The greatest joy was my newfound peace, which was greater than I had ever experienced. My spirit danced and was free to fully blossom. Today, I can clearly hear the whisper of the Holy Spirit and know the importance of allowing myself to be still so that I can truly receive and experience Him. After just a few short weeks of daily devotion I felt whole again and was fully experiencing His greatness, love, and mercy.

My experience has been one that is all too real in the lives of many everyday people just like me who get stuck in the middle of saint and sin. That day in July 2007, when I started my journal, I felt so broken, lost, alone, and spiritually empty. I am confident that I am not the only one that has been in that dark place. As you are reading, there may be a void that you have been seeking to fill. You are missing something and have been tirelessly running around this world in circles, trying to locate it.

My friend, I am here to tell you that what you are seeking does not lie within another living being, material possession, degree, or career. You have to redirect all of that time and energy towards building and maintaining your relationship with God. That love, peace, approval, confidence, companionship, and everything else that you are seeking, all lies within Him. You may be thinking, "Yeah, yeah, that's easier said than done." Listen to me. It can be done—one step and one day at a time. By taking just a few minutes daily to enter into God's presence, I promise that your life will be transformed. You can do it! For me, waking up early before starting my busy day really worked because it was an uninterrupted time and it set the tone for my day. You determine the time that works best for you and your schedule.

"Dawn of a New Day" captures my personal reflections during the first few weeks of my spiritual journey. After going back later to read over my entries, I found them to be profound and inspiring and believed them to be words of inspiration and encouragement from God. After much prayer, my spirit directed me to share these messages with you, so I simply gathered my initial entries and rewrote them to help you apply the passages to your own life. I have also shared a daily "Dawn's Diamond," which are small jewels to help you practice self-love by embracing and appreciating the simple joys of life.

My hope is that as you read the scriptures and motivational spiritual reflections, you become inspired and listen to your spirit so that you can receive the personal messages that God has for you. Take this time to build your relationship with Him, ignite your faith, and to discover His purpose and will for your life. It is time for a new dawn, a new day, and a new you.

DAWN OF A NEW DAY

A 21-Day Inspirational Journal to
Renew Your Faith, Mind & Spirit

STARTING YOUR JOURNEY

The steps for starting your journey are quite simple. For the next 21 days, make a commitment to spend at least 15 minutes daily with this journal and our Heavenly Father. This time is meant to be enjoyable, so prepare breakfast—your morning coffee, or whatever you need to make it your own personal time that can easily be maintained. Begin each day by reading the scripture, followed by the inspirational message. Then simply close your eyes, be still, and hear from God. This is the most important part. Take your time to really savor the moment and soak it all in. This is when you really get to hear from Him. Use this moment to really clear your mind of all thoughts, take deep breaths in and out, and listen from within. This may take five minutes or it could take twenty-five minutes. However long, take your time and simply enjoy being in His presence.

Once you are ready, write your thoughts and feelings in this journal. This is a place to record your personal reflections. When you have completed capturing your thoughts, take a moment to read over them allowing them to resonate within your soul. Secondly, think of all the ways God has blessed you. This can range from earning an advanced degree to getting a front parking spot at the grocery store. No matter how big or small, write it down and give God praise. Lastly, take some time to think of all the ways you need God to move in your life and in the life of others. Write down these prayer requests and truly just give them all over to Him. Now take a few deep breaths, in and out, and simply smile. While you are in sync with the Holy Spirit, go to a sacred place—whether it is in your bedroom, closet, living room, bathroom, car, or cubicle—and spend time in prayer.

When you are finished, slowly open your eyes, speak some words of thanks, and begin your day feeling renewed, refreshed, and rejuvenated. It's that simple. You will have started a new day in a peaceful place and opened your spirit to receive and give blessings throughout your day. You will experience a sense of peace, and feel the Holy Spirit stirring inside of you. The way you react to certain situations will be different and people will notice a light shining from within you. You will feel whole again. Stick to this daily devotional routine and watch as your thoughts and actions are transformed. Because this journal is compiled of my personal journal entries, you will be able to witness firsthand my transformation in my messages to you while you witness your own.

"Dawn of a New Day" is just the beginning of what will be an amazing and ever-evolving spiritual journey and relationship with God. My prayer is that He transforms you like He did me, and that you become inspired to become the person you have been designed to be, so that you can live your best life today, filled with happiness, love, peace, and joy.

DAY 1

"Therefore I say to you, whatever things you ask when you pray, believe that you receive them, and you will have them." **Mark 11:24**

You may be experiencing very trying times— emotionally and spiritually. This scripture will give you comfort in knowing that your prayers have not gone unnoticed, and that the Lord has delayed His response to your prayers for a purpose. There is a blessing in store for you, so just continue to trust in the power of God and stay diligent in your quest to be closer to Him. Pray for guidance and direction. Your biggest battle has been listening. Although you may have been disobedient, continue to have faith and know that it is not too late to live the life that God has specifically designed for you.

CLOSE YOUR EYES, BE STILL, AND HEAR FROM GOD.

TIFFANEY DALE

Personal Reflection:

DAWN OF A NEW DAY

PRAISES:

PRAYER REQUESTS:

TIFFANEY DALE

Dawn's Diamond

Light an array of scented candles and play soft music, while soaking in a hot bath filled with enriching bath salts and bubbles.

DAY 2

"My brethren, count it all joy when you fall into various trials, knowing that the testing of your faith produces patience. But let patience have its perfect work, that you may be perfect and complete, lacking nothing." **JAMES 1:2-4**

Appreciate that during trying times, you are simply being prepared for overcoming many of life's obstacles that lie ahead. Many adversaries will come your way, but you must remain faithful and pray that your foundation is solid and strong enough to endure the storms.

You will make it through. So, go ahead and praise God for all of the challenges that He sends your way because He will supply you with provisions to conquer them all. Have peace in knowing that your life of faith and triumphs will become part of your legacy, which will inspire the hearts and minds of others for many generations to come. Whether you know it or not, there is always someone watching and admiring you from a distance, so strive to be a great example by honoring and fulfilling God's purpose in all aspects of your life.

CLOSE YOUR EYES, BE STILL, AND HEAR FROM GOD.

TIFFANEY DALE

Personal Reflection:

DAWN OF A NEW DAY

PRAISES:
_____
_____
_____
_____
_____
_____
_____
_____
_____
_____

PRAYER REQUESTS:
_____
_____
_____
_____
_____
_____
_____
_____
_____

TIFFANEY DALE

Dawn's Diamond

Lift your spirits by listening and singing to Christian music by artists like Anthony Evans, Brian Courtney Wilson, Chris Tomlin, Fred Hammond, Hillsong United, Lecrae, and Matthew West.

DAY 3

"Now faith is the substance of things hoped for, the evidence of things not seen." **HEBREWS 11:1**

As a Christian early in their walk, many long to see a "burning bush." You know that, "If this is really you God, show me fill in the blank." Many want to experience a goosebumps and hair raising type of relationship with God because that is what they believe having faith and a spiritual relationship means. Well, that is not the case. Faith in God is about confidently trusting and believing in Him and all of His promises without seeing. Walk by faith and not by sight. Continue to trust in God and all of the promises that He has for you and know that every step that you take in life is ordered and directed by Him. Trust Him to lead you to a place of contentment, peace, and happiness. Stay strong and diligent in your new faith journey and make every new decision based on His will. Be encouraged. Simply trust. Simply believe.

CLOSE YOUR EYES, BE STILL, AND HEAR FROM GOD.

TIFFANEY DALE

Personal Reflection:

PRAISES:

PRAYER REQUESTS:

TIFFANEY DALE

DAWN'S DIAMOND

Enjoy a morning walk, run, or bike ride outdoors, while appreciating the many sights, sounds, and smells of nature.

DAY 4

"The Lord is slow to anger and great in power, and will not at all acquit the wicked. The LORD has His way in the whirlwind and in the storm, and the clouds are the dust of His feet." **NAHUM 1:3**

Like a hurricane or tornado swirling through a quiet town, there will be many unexpected storms that will turn your life completely upside down. During these traumatic times, it is easy to feel discouraged and helpless; however, you have been built to weather the storm. No matter how big or how long, if you depend on Him, you will make it through to the other side where you will discover more blessings, faith and awareness of His presence. The storms of life help you fully appreciate your many joys and blessings. Step back and just think about all that you have to be grateful for. Just think about it: you may have endured many storms in your relationships, business, finances, and family; however, in the end, each of your storms brought life to a new blessing. You are a flower that is blossoming, so pray that He continues to water your spirit through His presence and His Word.

CLOSE YOUR EYES, BE STILL, AND HEAR FROM GOD.

Personal Reflection:

PRAISES:

PRAYER REQUESTS:

TIFFANEY DALE

DAWN'S DIAMOND

Head over to your nearest Farmer's Market to shop for local products like fruits, vegetables, and homemade bath and beauty products.

DAY 5

"For I, the LORD your God, will hold thy right hand, saying to you, 'Fear not, I will help you.'" **ISAIAH 41:13**

Fear. Anxiety. Worry. The heaviness and darkness that comes with those emotions can be a constant grey cloud hovering over your every thought and decision. Let it go and let the soothing words of God become the source of your peace, calm, and confidence. Depend on Him and know that what you are battling is not bigger than your God. He will protect you. You are never alone. He is right by your side, clasping your hand, and guiding you along a path that He has carved out just for you. Stand up straight, lift your head, and walk confidently into your destiny.

CLOSE YOUR EYES, BE STILL, AND HEAR FROM GOD.

Personal Reflection:

Praises:

Prayer Requests:

TIFFANEY DALE

DAWN'S 💎 DIAMOND

Become inspired through the creative works of artists by touring local art galleries and museums.

DAY 6

"... and being fully convinced that what He had promised He was also able to perform." **ROMANS 4:21**

God fulfills all of His promises. If He said it and placed the desire in your heart, He will do it. Have faith in His miraculous ways and you will soon witness firsthand how He makes His glorious presence known in every aspect of your life. Whether it is personal, professional, or physical, God wants the best for you. So, continue to move forward by believing in His marvelous promises and plans that will soon be revealed to you.

CLOSE YOUR EYES, BE STILL, AND HEAR FROM GOD.

TIFFANEY DALE

Personal Reflection:

PRAISES:

PRAYER REQUESTS:

TIFFANEY DALE

DAWN'S DIAMOND

Pick or purchase some fresh flowers and place them in vases throughout your home and office space.

Day 7

"My brethren, count it all joy when you fall into various trials, knowing that the testing of your faith produces patience. But let patience have its perfect work, that you may be perfect and complete, lacking nothing." **JAMES 1:2-4**

Lacking patience will result in many of the stresses and trials that you face today. Rather than waiting on God, you allow your personal desires and the perspectives of others to influence your actions and beliefs. Please wait patiently and recognize that the Lord has great plans for you, so let His work and will be done. No matter what you are facing, He knows, so just trust Him. Read your bible, marinate on His Word, and watch as He slowly reveals His desires for you. Rest in the Lord and be patient. There is power in the "wait" so just be still. Your breakthrough and blessings are on the way.

CLOSE YOUR EYES, BE STILL, AND HEAR FROM GOD.

TIFFANEY DALE
Personal Reflection:

PRAISES:

PRAYER REQUESTS:

TIFFANEY DALE

DAWN'S ♥ DIAMOND

Enjoy the meditative experience of chopping fresh ingredients and cooking healthy and nourishing meals for the entire week.

DAY 8

"Be anxious for nothing, but in everything by prayer and supplication, with thanksgiving, let your requests be made known to God." **PHILIPPIANS 4:6**

When things are moving along great in your life, it is easy to shout Hallelujah and give God praise. But what about when things are chaotic and nothing seems to be going your way? Prayer and praise; that's right. There is so much power in prayer, so redirect your focus from your problems and look up towards the heavens. No matter how big or small, just give it all to Him. Share your every concern, want, need, and desire and be assured that your prayers are not falling on deaf ears. They are all being answered in God's timing, so be patient. Answers to your prayers are on the way, so stay hopeful and prayerful and know that if it is His will, it will be done!

CLOSE YOUR EYES, BE STILL, AND HEAR FROM GOD.

TIFFANEY DALE
Personal Reflection:

DAWN OF A NEW DAY

PRAISES:

PRAYER REQUESTS:

DAWN'S DIAMOND

Soothe your mind and soul by listening to classical music from legendary composers such as Bach, Chopin, Schumann, Tchaikovsky, and Vivaldi.

DAY 9

"No temptation has overtaken you except such as is common to man; but God is faithful, who will not allow you to be tempted beyond what you are able, but with the temptation will also make the way of escape, that you may be able to bear it." **1 CORINTHIANS 10:13**

Regardless of what you may encounter, God will never leave your side. Your prayer should be to have continued strength and commitment to cultivating a relationship with Him without drifting away as you have in the past. You may have a few setbacks, which is not uncommon when you are on the right path and living according to His Word. So, when you feel yourself slipping back into old ways, remember the overwhelming feeling of comfort and peace that you experience while basking in His presence. As long as you are breathing, you will endure temptations, but always remember that you have an almighty power living within you that is bigger and stronger than any temptation that you will ever face.

CLOSE YOUR EYES, BE STILL, AND HEAR FROM GOD.

TIFFANEY DALE

Personal Reflection:

DAWN OF A NEW DAY

PRAISES:

PRAYER REQUESTS:

TIFFANEY DALE

DAWN'S DIAMOND

Get your body moving and try something new like ballroom dancing, barre, martial arts, soul cycle, or yoga.

DAY 10

"Trust in the Lord with all your heart, and lean not on your own understanding." **PROVERBS 3:5**

Are you being held hostage to the pains, sorrows, and regrets of your past? Let them go and trust in the Lord with all of your heart. Release them and set them free. Once you get rid of all of the heaviness that has weighed you down, you will finally heal. Trust in Him and realize that you are not defined by your past or the opinions of others. Like a leaf floating down a flowing stream, let it all flow away and let the Holy Spirit lead you into a realm of love, peace, joy, and happiness.

CLOSE YOUR EYES, BE STILL, AND HEAR FROM GOD.

TIFFANEY DALE
Personal Reflection:

DAWN OF A NEW DAY

PRAISES:

PRAYER REQUESTS:

TIFFANEY DALE

DAWN'S ♥ DIAMOND

Feel like a carefree kid again by spending an afternoon daydreaming, swinging, and flying a kite in a park.

DAY 11

"O LORD, You have searched me and known me. You know my sitting down and my rising up; You understand my thought afar off. You comprehend my path and my lying down, And are acquainted with all my ways." **PSALM 139:1-3**

The many events that transpire in your life and thoughts that cross your mind are no surprise to God. He knows and sees it all. So there is never any need to hide from Him because you are ashamed of having made some bad choices. He knew your path before you ever walked it, so shake away your shame. You are a beautiful child of God who is loved and forgiven. Nothing that you have gone through or will go through is without a purpose, so just trust in Him. He will never give you more than you can handle, so just embrace this vulnerable, yet sacred place that you are in.

CLOSE YOUR EYES, BE STILL, AND HEAR FROM GOD.

TIFFANEY DALE

Personal Reflection:

DAWN OF A NEW DAY

PRAISES:

PRAYER REQUESTS:

TIFFANEY DALE

DAWN'S DIAMOND

Spend a day in loungewear watching favorite movies from your childhood, while munching on an assortment of candy, ice cream, pizza, and popcorn.

DAY 12

"But it will turn out for you as an occasion for testimony."
LUKE 21:13

You are a walking and living testimony. Every trial and tribulation you experience is an opportunity to share just how good God is to you. Because He will never forsake you. Like the old adage says, "He may not come when you want Him, but He will come right on time." So during trying times, rest in knowing that God is transforming you into someone greater and when it is time, He will open the way for you to bless the life of others by sharing your testimony of how He worked in your life. If He did it for you, He will do it for others.

CLOSE YOUR EYES, BE STILL, AND HEAR FROM GOD.

TIFFANEY DALE

Personal Reflection:

DAWN OF A NEW DAY

PRAISES:

_____
_____
_____
_____
_____
_____
_____
_____
_____
_____

PRAYER REQUESTS:

_____
_____
_____
_____
_____
_____
_____
_____
_____

TIFFANEY DALE

DAWN'S DIAMOND

Treat yourself to a local live music performance and sing and dance like you are the headlining performer.

DAY 13

"But let him who glories glory in this, That he understands and knows Me, That I am the LORD, exercising loving kindness, judgement, and righteousness in the earth. For in these I delight," says the LORD." **JEREMIAH 9:24**

From a new car and a new job to a new relationship and a new wardrobe, many often find themselves searching the world for acceptance and validation. That type of life is often filled with emptiness, confusion, and disappointment. From this day forward, look to God to satisfy your needs and stop placing value on material things and expectations. You will discover that there is so much more pleasure in the simple joys of life. Live accordingly to His Word and will. Care only about the things that are from Him and ask Him to transform you into an extraordinary Christian.

CLOSE YOUR EYES, BE STILL, AND HEAR FROM GOD.

TIFFANEY DALE
Personal Reflection:

PRAISES:

_____
_____
_____
_____
_____
_____
_____
_____
_____
_____

PRAYER REQUESTS:

_____
_____
_____
_____
_____
_____
_____
_____
_____
_____

TIFFANEY DALE

DAWN'S DIAMOND

Purchase some art supplies and let your creativity and imagination run wild with some paint and a blank canvas.

DAY 14

"Jesus answered and said to him, "What I am doing you do not understand now, but you will know after this." **JOHN 13:7**

The hurt and pain of losing someone or something that you have valued and poured so much of your time and energy into can literally bring you down to your knees. The grief that comes with a broken bond becomes so unbearable that you find yourself calling out in despair, "Why is this happening to me?" Well your answer lies here in John 13:7. Knowing this truth, your cry of despair should now become shouts of praise! Be thankful; God will break you away from toxic people, unhealthy situations, and dependency on others to mold you into the Christian that He desires for you to be. It may be painful to go through this "chopping" process, but be assured that He has great plans in store for you.

CLOSE YOUR EYES, BE STILL, AND HEAR FROM GOD.

TIFFANEY DALE

Personal Reflection:

PRAISES:

PRAYER REQUESTS:

DAWN'S ♥ DIAMOND

Pamper yourself with a day at the spa and lounge in the sauna and steam room before indulging in treatments like a massage, facial, mud bath, or body scrub.

Day 15

"Bring all the tithes into the storehouse, that there may be food in My house, and try Me now in this," says the LORD of hosts, "If I will not open for you the windows of heaven, and pour out for you such blessing, that there will not be room enough to receive it." **MALACHI 3:10**

There is a late rent notice on the door. The car payment is several months behind. Credit collectors are calling daily and each day you go home you are praying that when you flip up the switch, the lights come on. Sound familiar? If you have some difficult financial times and have spent many restless nights overcome by worry, I encourage you to step out on faith and tithe 10 percent of your earnings and watch God transform your situation. Do your part by supporting His Kingdom and you can trust and believe that He will abundantly supply all of your financial needs.

CLOSE YOUR EYES, BE STILL, AND HEAR FROM GOD.

TIFFANEY DALE

Personal Reflection:

PRAISES:

PRAYER REQUESTS:

TIFFANEY DALE

DAWN'S ♦ DIAMOND

Snuggle up with a good book or magazine that you would normally only read while away on vacation.

DAY 16

"This is My commandment, that you love one another as I have loved you." **JOHN 15:12**

Love does not cost you a single penny, so why not just give it out freely and openly? Tear down the walls that have been built because of past hurts and pains and follow the Lord's commandment to love others as He loves you. It is that simple, so stop right now to think about all of the people who are in your life. From family and friends to neighbors and colleagues, begin to express and show your love. Share with them how much they mean to you with kind gestures like a phone call, text message, email, or sweet note. You will brighten their day, while feeling great in the process so slow down and make time for all those who bring purpose and meaning to your existence. There is no promise that tomorrow will ever come, so let them know today.

CLOSE YOUR EYES, BE STILL, AND HEAR FROM GOD.

TIFFANEY DALE

Personal Reflection:

PRAISES:

PRAYER REQUESTS:

DAWN'S ♥ DIAMOND

Blast songs by your favorite music artists, get in front of a mirror and show off your best dance moves.

DAY 17

"So he shepherded them according to the integrity of his heart, and guided them by the skillfulness of his hands." **PSALM 78:72**

Imagine gliding through the golden doors of a majestic castle that is filled to capacity with sparkly wrapped packages draped with shimmering red bows. As you look closer, you discover that your name has been engraved on each and every one of these splendid gifts. There are glorious destinations where God wants to take you that consist of countless gifts and blessings. But you must follow His guidance rather than attempting to follow your own path. The more you listen to self rather than Him, the longer it will take you to get to where He intended for you to be all along. Let your prayer be to have the ability to listen and follow His direction—to be obedient to Him. Simply take His hand and follow His guidance along this magical journey of life.

CLOSE YOUR EYES, BE STILL, AND HEAR FROM GOD.

TIFFANEY DALE
Personal Reflection:

Praises:

_____
_____
_____
_____
_____
_____
_____
_____
_____
_____

Prayer Requests:

_____
_____
_____
_____
_____
_____
_____
_____
_____
_____

TIFFANEY DALE

DAWN'S DIAMOND

Treasure yourself by planning a staycation at a luxurious hotel and dining at an upscale restaurant.

DAY 18

"And He said unto me, 'My grace is sufficient for you, for My strength is made perfect in weakness.' Therefore most gladly I will rather boast in my infirmities, that the power of Christ may rest upon me." **2 CORINTHIANS 12:9**

Live each day fully knowing that God's will and grace are sufficient enough for you. Live with contentment and be thankful for all things. Thank God for all that He is doing and will continue to do in your life. Be grateful for His power and presence! Thank Him for blessing you with family, friends, clients, cars, home, food, utilities, time, flexibility, motivation, health, mind, peace, faith, hope, dreams, laughter, love, tears, experiences, personality, life, luxuries, clothing… EVERYTHING! Give God thanks for all of the golden treasures that He has created especially for you. Be grateful that He is at the center of it all.

CLOSE YOUR EYES, BE STILL, AND HEAR FROM GOD.

TIFFANEY DALE

Personal Reflection:

DAWN OF A NEW DAY

PRAISES:

_____
_____
_____
_____
_____
_____
_____
_____
_____
_____

PRAYER REQUESTS:

_____
_____
_____
_____
_____
_____
_____
_____
_____
_____

TIFFANEY DALE

DAWN'S DIAMOND

Broaden your mind by enrolling in a conversational foreign language class like Spanish, Italian, or French.

DAY 19

"Watch, stand fast in the faith, be brave, be strong."
1 CORINTHIANS 16:13

There is no situation that God cannot fix or get you through. Believe in His power and be grateful that you are now beginning to live your life in accordance with Him and His Word. Everything is possible with and through Him, so have faith in all the things and circumstances that come your way. He will guide you through them all. Remain strong in your faith as you face daily struggles. You have become stronger spiritually and emotionally and equipped with tools to begin making better decisions for your life—decisions that will glorify Him and His Kingdom. So confidently continue to march along this journey and remain steadfast in becoming a new you.

CLOSE YOUR EYES, BE STILL, AND HEAR FROM GOD.

TIFFANEY DALE

Personal Reflection:

DAWN OF A NEW DAY

PRAISES:

_____
_____
_____
_____
_____
_____
_____
_____
_____
_____
_____

PRAYER REQUESTS:

_____
_____
_____
_____
_____
_____
_____
_____
_____
_____

DAWN'S ♥ DIAMOND

Give selflessly of your time, talent, and treasures by serving as a volunteer in the community.

DAY 20

"And the LORD God said, "It is not good that the man should be alone; I will make him a helper comparable to him."
GENESIS 2:18

Value this time you have had alone to hear God's voice and learn His lessons. If you are single, be grateful for this time and know that it is not intended to be for a lifetime. Apply the wisdom you have gained during this time of devotion when choosing who you allow in your space. The bar has been raised so be wise and refuse to settle for anything or anyone that is not in line with the life that God wants for you. Know that you will never be able to fulfill any need of loneliness or companionship on your own. So, while daydreaming about Mr. or Mrs. Right, you must remember that you are in the earthly realm and that no one will fulfill you the way God can. He and only He can fulfill all of your needs.

CLOSE YOUR EYES, BE STILL, AND HEAR FROM GOD.

TIFFANEY DALE
Personal Reflection:

Praises:

_____
_____
_____
_____
_____
_____
_____
_____
_____
_____

Prayer Requests:

_____
_____
_____
_____
_____
_____
_____
_____
_____
_____

TIFFANEY DALE

DAWN'S ♥ DIAMOND

Explore the world from the comforts of home by flipping through the pages of travel magazines, which may even inspire you to plan an adventurous trip.

DAY 21

"To know the love of Christ which passes knowledge; that you may be filled with all the fullness of God." **EPHESIANS 3:19**

Thank God for loving you. Savor this time of devotion with your Heavenly Father and treasure this sacred and intimate time that you two have been sharing. You may have been yearning for love, peace, and joy from the world, but what you have been longing for has been available to you all along—by being in His presence. Do not stray, but remain close, focused and obedient. Power forward along your new path because there is an abundance of miraculous lessons, wisdom and blessings that await you. Be strong and content with this new direction in which you are headed. Many great things are in store for you so just rejoice and give Him thanks!

CLOSE YOUR EYES, BE STILL, AND HEAR FROM GOD.

TIFFANEY DALE

Personal Reflection:

PRAISES:

_____

PRAYER REQUESTS:

_____

DAWN'S ♥ DIAMOND

Keep your spiritual tank full by staying immersed in His Word by reading empowerment books and by listening to inspirational audio books in your car during daily commutes.

"If we confess our sins, He is faithful and just to forgive us our sins, and cleanse us from all unrighteousness." **1 John 1:9**

Surrender it all to God. Everything. You are flawed and have not been perfect along this journey. No one is perfect and that is okay. Simply confess and repent for all of your sins. Bow humbly before Him and allow Him to shower you with His grace and mercy. Remember, you are being chiseled into the person God wants you to be. Every situation you are placed in is preparing you for completion. Every circumstance is part of His process so be confident in knowing that through your trials, God will bring you through, while using it as a teaching opportunity. You will come out stronger, wiser, and better prepared to tackle the next trial that comes your way. You have come a long way, but will always be a work in progress so just embrace every step of this amazing journey.

My prayer is that you have been blessed abundantly throughout these 21 days and that you have discovered a new and enriching relationship with your Heavenly Father. By spending just a few minutes each day to speak to and hear from Him, your faith, mind, and spirit will be constantly renewed. I encourage you to continue along this journey by reading biblical scriptures, reflecting on His Word, writing down your praises and prayer requests each day, and discovering your own "Dawn's Diamonds." You have come too far to turn back now, so embrace this spiritual voyage as you embark on a new dawn and a new day, while continuously discovering a new you!

Love, Peace, and Blessings,

Tiffaney Dale

About the Author

Tiffaney Dale is an award-winning business owner, philanthropist, speaker, and author, who gives selflessly of her time, talent, and treasures to empower and uplift the lives of others.

A highly respected and trusted industry and business pioneer, Tiffaney is the heart and brain behind **Tiffaney Dale Agency**, a full-service public relations and marketing company that has been successfully placing brands in national media outlets and marketing platforms since 2006. She has received an array of awards and accolades and has served on the board of directors for several organizations. Additionally, through her motivational speaking series, Tiffaney enjoys inspiring audiences with her testimonies of transforming life's many obstacles into successes.

Moreover, as the founder of the **Dallas Hunter** and the **Houston Hunter** lifestyle blogs, she cultivates her passion for writing, while enlightening readers about an array of topics including art, travel, fashion, and dining.

A graduate of the University of North Texas, Tiffaney received the coveted Distinguished Young Alumnus of the Year award in 2015 and established the **Hunter Newton Legacy Endowment**, a $25,000 scholarship honoring her family's legacy of entrepreneurship, philanthropy, and education for qualifying students enrolled at the University of North Texas.

Tiffaney currently resides in Dallas, Texas where she is a member of Oak Cliff Bible Fellowship with Senior Pastor Dr. Tony Evans. She is pursuing an MBA at Southern Methodist University's Cox School of Business.

Learn more by visiting www.TiffaneyDale.com.

CONTACT INFORMATION
Tiffaney Dale Agency
2201 Main Street, Suite 785
Dallas, Texas 75201
Phone: 888.767.9765
Email: info@tiffaneydale.com

CHARITABLE DONATIONS
A percentage of book sales will be donated to selected organizations and to the Hunter Newton Legacy Endowment.

SPECIAL APPEARANCES
Please submit book signing and speaker requests to info@tiffaneydale.com.

STAY CONNECTED
Facebook: @tiffaneydaleagency
Instagram: @tiffaneydale
Twitter: @tiffaneydale
YouTube: Tiffaney Dale Agency

Made in the USA
Lexington, KY
06 November 2019

Made in the USA
Las Vegas, NV
21 October 2023

SUBMIT YOUR OWN FAKE BIBLE VERSE

FAKEBIBLEVERSES.COM

✝

And then shall be the time of wailing, of the gnashing of teeth, and of the smearing of jam.

Toddlers 2:3

And the Lord shall smite thy persecutors and cause their bowels-parts to drag behind them like defective weather balloons for the rest of their days.

Vengeances 25:13

✝

Know thyself through the likes of many.

Selfies 10:1

To every hand there is a season. A time to hold, a time to fold, a time of walking and a time in which thou must flee.

Gamblers 3:16

✝

An eye for an eye is good for
the optometrists.

Postmoderns 5:17

For my snufflings cometh
before I eat, and my snottings
are poured out like the
waters.

Allergies 24:7

✝

For only he who posesseth thy pop and lock, who robot eth and moonwalk eth, and windmill eth and Toprock, shall saveth thy miracles from the temptations of the adversary.

Boogaloo 19:84

For only he who hath
surviveth thy mapless maze,
and muled thy load within,
shall receiveth thy glorious
prize of toil, puzzled wood
and wrench

Ikeas 7:23

✝

For only when thou hath received tortuous screams of many and thy dishes hath been flung upon thy walls wilt thou understandeth thy transgression.

Companions 9:8

And though thou shall wail and bellow unto the tiny speaker, thou shalt not be bequeathed thy order of burger, soda and tasty fries. A fish sandwich and tea of unsweetness shall be delivered unto thee.

Drive-Thrus 24:7

✝

And he broke the bread and spread upon it the churned milk of the mayonnaise tree.

Condiments 16:3

But what if he stumbles, or
trips, or falls, or skins his little
knee, or catches cold, or eats
something off the ground and
contracteth a fungus of the
lip?

Hysterics 9:11

✝

Hear me not?? Less THOU SHALL SAY with great COMMAND!!!! Lest ye not heed my word now!!!!!!

Exclamations 7:1

It is I who sayeth the word for
the word that is said be from
I who who sayeth the word
for the word that is said ... Be
from I.

Repetitions 3:3:3:3:3

✝

Then were they curs'd. Forced
to live by the sweat of brow,
the grease of hands, the turn
of wrench and the pad of
estimates.

Mechanics 7:15

And cause the slow and mis-shapened among you to be taken to the unclean place of the city and cast in a pit with the refuse and potsherds.

Eugenics 3:17

✝

Adam hath spake to Eve,
What hath caused thy
furrowed brow? Nothing twas
the only reply. And without
word, much was said. A
darkness filled Adam's heart.

Matrimonies 9:12

Knoweth this, though I now
lay dutifully at your feet, I
shall play and frolic with
much vigor on thy bed whilst
thee are out.

Canines 4:23

✝

The number of the taking
shall be two and the time of
calling shall be the morning.

Physicians 5:1

So they would know love, unconditional, did the Lord did bless them with Dog. And when they got uppity about the whole thing, he sent Cat to put them in their place.

Companions 27:3

✝

I am that I was but not what I
will be hence that I was once
before being.

Confusions 2:15

Nay! For shall I knoweth thy answer upon sight.

Clients 8:237

✝

In the East, a strange land of people who are yet too cool even for themselves. The damned name it Brooklyn.

Hipsters 1:1

Whatever hideous beast of baked earth thou shall bring unto the world, shall thy family receiveth reluctantly and with great begrudge.

Ceramics 1:01

✝

Account of thyself, sinner! For each packet of sauce thou must make testament and confession unto the window.

Drive-Thrus 2:12

For only if ye hath somite and antennae and mandible and maxillae shall ye truly know the ocean floor.

Crustaceans 12:7

✝

I foresaw your coming as I peer'd out my window, and thus girded my loins again your tolling of the bell. But nay, O witness of Jehovah, I shall not answer for I hath secured refuge behind couch in hopes that ye shall pass on.

Solicitations 2:25

Mark this and mark it well, spake Gabriel, When thou rest upon a porcelain throne at thy place of daily toil, remember to leave one stall betwixt thyself and thy fellow toilers' throne, for this is the space of the blessed.

Etiquettes 1:2

✝

It shall come to pass that in the thirteenth year, humanity will no longer reside within thee, and not until the hormonal tempest hath passed, wilt thou or thy elders see it again

Adolescents 1:1

The work to which ye are
called cannot be subscribed to
without the work of it, yet
you cannot get the job of it
without you have already
done the work.

Absurdities 16:9

✝

No one shall tell a navy man when he has had enough to drink. For onliest shall the man of the waters have the knowledge of the limits of his own drinking.

Drunkards 7:7

Then did the Lord create the seas and all creatures within; fishes of one and two, then thus of red and blue. Yea, and though some beith sad, others shall be glad and few will be very, very bad.

Book of Seuss 3:1

✝

Thou shall not pay retail.

Hipsters 2:1

In the latter days, beasts of no talent and large humps shall be born unto your family. And, for this reason, gold, and rare gifts from unwise men will be showered upon your house.

Kardashians 8:23

✝

For none shall deduct thy
meals except he who travels
for thy work

Expenses 8:7

The robe to helle is paved
with auto-correction.

iPhones 8:3

✝

And Moab spake unto
Jebehosethah.. And
Jebehosethah cried out unto
his mother, saying Mother.
'Moab is spaking on me
again'

Book of Noises 18:4

The profligate son returns.

Post-graduates 5:15

✝

If thou must ask, thou canst afford it

Elitists 12:2

The leftest was made for those who are swift of pace and heavy of foot. If thine ass and cart be slow do not tarry there, for it is a sin, and they shall be right to maketh rude gestures in thine mirror.

Drivers I-95

✝

And the world did shake, and thy nylon maidens fled, and the voice above speaketh to all for lo, the time of belts was upon us!!!

Turbulence 4:2

Thou shalt quit in wrathful
protest when thine special,
special head is not anointed
with the oil of abundant
praise.

Millennials 2:5

✝

Yea, though my love is great for you, I grow weary of your slothfulness each morn. For there are teeth to be brush'd, hair to be comb'd, clothes to be dress'd and breakfast to be eat'd. But nay, I must use ox and mule to drag thee from thy place of slumber.

Adolescents 13:2

And the Lord said unto the DJ of the Snake. Indeed, wherefore should I turn down? And for what?

Inanities 17:2

✝

And Abraham said unto the male servants of his house, Now shall ye be circumsiz'd as the Lord hath commanded. And thus answered the servants, Now can ye can taketh this job and place it where thy Lord does not allow the sun to shine! And Abraham said, but ye are bondservants unto this house and will do as ye are told. I own thee, even the bits that will be chopp'd off from thee, those still will still I own.

And her wailings shall pour
forth like the ocean, even
though all is right in heaven
and upon the earth.

Lamentations 1:7

✝

Thus it is written; there shall
be precious little time to do
thy job, but copious amounts
to maketh changes.

Book of Clients 1:1

Thy can still covet thy OWN ox and donkey, just not thy neighbor's.

Clarifications 7:2

✝

Those who spake much and loudly of their love for the Lord often have much hidden in their shadows. Keep a steady watch on thy back.

Skeletons 5:13

Thou shall wait hours of
many for words of few.

Physicians 8:25

✝

Seek not to knoweth whose
fault it was. The fault is thine.

Blames 7:7

Thou shall not commit adulthood.

Descendants 19:83

✝

It is foretold, thou shalt be only ones to succeed without the blessing of talent, the sweat of brow, or the benefit of experience.

Millennials 12:17

Thou art entrapped and
unable to walk free. The
reason, sayeth the Elvis, is
love. You have no eyes with
which to see. No belief with
which to trust. There will be
no continuance in the face of
such superstition.

Elvises 3:21

✝

Behold, though thy face hath been painted gruesome and thy robes be of black and spike, ye cannot be truly 'metal' without screech of solo and burst of many flames.

Book of Simmons 6:6:6

And the LORD commanded
man, Thou are freeth to eat
from any tree in the garden;
but thy country-style buffet
shall surely offer ye more
selection.

Seniors 6 a.m.

✝

And on this day thy Heavenly
Father shall say unto thee,
Halloha!

Salutations 1:1

And yea, listen unto me,
child. Though the Charms
give you great joy, tis but
fleeting, for the Lucky is truly
part of thy balanced breakfast.

Cereals 7:15

✝

Thy Terms of Use (Terms) of thy word shall govern thy accessth or use by thy, from within earth and its territories and possessions of animals, and plants and seas (the Blessings) made available in thy Earth and its territories and possessions by thy LORD and its subsidiaries and affiliates.

Conditions 7:2

Thy tiny suit shall squeeze thy
brain to shrink so thy beard
can run amok.

Hipsters 2:88

✝

All that can go wrong has gone wrong lest ye be able to prove otherwise.

Murphies 9:32

For it shall be easier for a camel to pass through the eye of a needle, than for a businessman to enter the kingdom of flight.

Transportations 2:10

✝

I liketh not thy coffee in heaven. Thou must improveth the grind of thy holy bean.

Suggestions 4:4

And when my legs have failed me he brought unto me a chair with wheels. And when the way grew steep, he hath provided the elevator.

Invalids 9:21

✝

As the penitent musician
kneels before the score and
whispers, 'Every good boy
deserveth fudge.'

Mnemonics 4:4

By the magic of pricing shall
he turn shit to gold.

Coupons 10:20

✝

And then did the people smile and make merriment, while within their secret hearts they did judge and grumble.

Holidays 4:11

So the Lord sayeth unto ye
about what the Lord hath
sayeth the lest ye not
remember

Quotations 8:8

✝

Oh Heavenly Father, Please findth enclosed mine CV for the post of disciple. Great is mine admiration and praise for your heavenly organization and what thy in thy strategic mercy hath done with thy earth. Also, I have previous experience with fishing.

Applications 7:3

Spake the wrench'd, 'Ensurest thou that the heated water and the unheated water come not together, and that the feverish water be not on the right, and that effluent rolleth unto the lowest places of the land.'

Plumbers 4:14-15

✝

Know this, if thou doth not believe solely as I then I shalt bellow loudly, casting down the fire of my word upon thee and thy followers until ye are blasted from the earth.

Hannitys 24:7, Medias 25:7, Inanities 3:5

If that which ye do does not discomfit thee, surely then no profit may come from it.

Athletics 1:3

✝

Cast ye cargo over fence! For it is I who chooseth not the open door.

Deliveries 10:17

For only a thirsty man who shall enterth without shoes, coat, belt or bag, who hath offered a sacrifice of sacred possessions unto the tiny tray shall enter the kingdom within.

Transportations 7:1

✝

Honor thy mother and thy father's table.

Doilies 6:1

Sew! sayeth the Lord.

Darnings 1:1

✝

'Will thou not learn a lesson and obey my words?' declared the LORD. Now bringeth my coffee.

Interns 7:21

Behold!, said the Master, I bring you a sphere of golden happiness! As he tossed it on high, the hound knew this to be true. For his soul ached to retrieve it in hopes that the Lord may toss it forth from this day unto the end of days

Canines 12:5

✝

In my youth, hath I made pilgrimage to gather knowledge each day born new. But my travels were frought with peril as I did hath to climb each way through many cubits of snow, unshodden.

Ruminations 7:8

Yea, for this is my noun, take of it and verb for it is glory in thine eyes and shall maketh thee adjective. Then upon the birth of the new day, kneel before thy noun and praise it on adjective!

Book of Libs 4:1

✝

And thus the Lord did smite the sack maker. For when he tried to open it, the fruit snacks of the Lord were tossed hither and thither.

Packages 4:12

Long hath thy child sought
thy colored egg for scramble,
poach or fry. And many
omelets layeth yet unfound.
Blessed be the BOILED egg
thy young hath found!

Bunnies 4:5

✝

Thou shall not krill.

Crustations 3:27

Lo, tho thy troubles number four score and nineteen, the Whore of Babylon is not among them

Jayz 6:4

✝

Thus the olde man spoke unto me, When we haveth no meat, we ateth fowl, when we duth haveth no fowl, we din'd' upon crustacean, and when we haveth no crustacean we feasth upon the sand. I did ask with earnest "You feastd upon sand?"" He answered, 'Yea, we feast'd upon sand.'

Cohens 1:25

When the Devil appeared to
Christ, wandering in the
desert, spake he, 'S'up.' and
thrusteth forth his forked
chin.

Salutations 25:3

✝

Wealth gotten by vanity shall be diminished but he that gathereth by labour shall be taxed at 48%.

Demotivations 7:14

And then a pestilence did descend upon the land. The rivers ran yellow and the beasts of the field choked and wheezed and cried out Allegra, Allegra! Hallelujah, Allegra!

Allergies 21:5

✝

The reckoning of man shall be divided according to the part of parts and the part of labor.

Mechanics 1:2

And even as ye struggle to manage pro-ject, they shall break timelines, creep scope and destroy work.

Clients 9:18

✝

And thus it was handed forth that on the third day all men shall offer the refuse of his house unto the curb.

Sanitations 3:3

The Lord is a shoving leopard,
I wall not shan't.

Spoonerisms 3:8

✝

In the land of metal, the one-arm'd drummer is king.

Hysterias 6:6, Leppards 1:13

Halt-footed and awkward in the place of shufflings and mumblings, cast thy gaze downward and shape to say, 'whatever.'

Adolescents 13:16

✝

Entereth the words
separatedeth only by a space
and shall you be reckoned
true.

Verifications 5:12

Nay, no potatoes, nor sacred
meats upon thy bread, only a
crispy fish. Why hath the
drive through forsaken me yet
again?

Clowns 5:3

✝

Preheat thy oven to three hundred and fifty of degrees. Only then shall thy shall mixeth thy beans into thy dish. Oh baketh thy beaneth for hours of three and then poureth thy beeney goodness upon thy plate! Rejoice, for thy task is done!

Directions 23:2

Blessed are those who spend more, for they shall inherit the kingdom of First Class.

Flights 8:34

✝

What sayeth thou? Hath thou belongings been withith thou for eternity? Hath thou accepted gifts from he who is not known?

Transportations 8:10

Oh whereth thine gold of plenty? For it is I who has been at task for hours of three.

Millennials 23

✝

Must thou receive the body of Christ alone? Neh! Haveth thou tried with the butter of nuts? The cheeses of cows? Or the many soups of our land?

Saltines 17:3

Protesteth all things my child,
for as ye nuzzle thy head
within my bearded pits, my
love of ye shall never be
washed.

Hippies 19:68

✝

Divideth thy unguents for
greater healing. If thy hurt be
great, divide and divide again.
By nothing shall something
be cured.

Homeopaths 3:19

When ye reacheth golden age
thou shall make pilgrimage to
a sacred land where thy bones
shall not be ache'd by cold,
thy grown child shan't haunt
thy dwelling and thy state
shall not taxeth thee, for I
hath created Florida.

Seniors 5:18

✝

Thus Abraham spoke unto his daughter. Yea, I shall take thy first boyfriend and smote him upon the mount to show unto others that thy father is righteous and shall not be trifled with!

Daughters 1:1

Nay! Judgeth not thy manhood, for thy water is cold!

Shrinkages 1:1

✝

If it is too loud, behold, thou
are ancient among men.

Reverbs 5:17

Ask, and it shall be given you; seek, and ye shall find; leave thy package outside, and it shall be stolen.

Deliveries 19:4

✝

The faster ye runs, the longer shall be thy awaiting delay.

Connections 1:100

That which time can not erase, thy ink can coverth.

Tattoos 7:6

✝

And the Lord did speak to the prophet, saying that his name shall be known as Foxtrot-Alpha-Tango-Hotel-Echo-Romeo. Then the Lord then maketh the sound Pkkkkk which we thinketh means the Lord of Hosts was done.

Pilots 5:24

Yea, for thou hath taken the
form of a hound and thy
wailings are long and
constant!

Elvises 19:56

✝

The number of carry-ons shall
be two, for three is a sin and
wrongful in thy Lord's eyes.
They shall be no larger than
can what be placed gently
below thy feet or risen above
in thy overhead.

Transportations 3:9

And shall ye cross thy street
without fear, sight, speed, or
regard for speeding carriages,
for I haveth THY right of way
and THAT maketh me
mighty with the Lord!

Pedestrians 6:2

✝

Lo, the Lord will visit thy face with oily pox, and hair shall he maketh to grow in strange places, and thy body shall be wracked with change.

Adolescents 2:1-3

Thou shalt wait in great
penance at the belted altar in
silence and contemplation,
for if thee hath been a good
and faithful passenger in the
Lord's eyes shall ye receive thy
luggage unblemished.

Transportations 10:13

✝

For it is written in the finest of print, thy shall receiveth thy one-day salvation in up to eleven weeks from the promised date.

Deliveries 17:2

The filth of thy habitation
being the fault, it is easier to
argue over than to remedy

Matrimonies 12:3

✝

All thy gold be mine if thou cansn't seek another's help in time of need

Mechanics 10:17

Unto me I see thy wandering masses with bow'd heads and faces cast in white glow. Yea, for they hath succumbd to a false pocket idol.

Jobs 1 4, 4s, 5, 5s, 6, 6-plus

✝

Thou shall knowth not of TV
speak for thou believeth not.

Hipsters 3:22

Thou shall not ha-ha!

Germans 2:44

✝

Yea, though thou will experience brief delights, ye must first be compressed with thy neighbor in a maze of iron that shall make ye wreak of sweat and cottoneth candy.

Amusements 4:1

Dareth thou stand? Thy
maidens of the sky shall strike
thee down lest ye buckle
before the light of belts.

Transportations 9:11

✝

And the Lord spake to warn the children. 'Steppest thou upon the crevasse, and surely thy mother's back shall yet be rent in twain.'

Superstitions 13:13

Yea, though I, he, she, we, they, thy, thou walk through the valley of the shadow of death, I, he, she, we, they, thy, thou will fear no evil.

Pronouns 6:22

✝

The opening of the first shall foretell the release of multitudes.

Fermentations 7:12

Oh Lord I thankth ye for all ye hath done for thy humble once-servant! This most unworthy of your once-children hath taken another savior and giveth, oh Lord, two weeks of note

Resignations 7:23, Apostates 1:1

✝

Yea, and though the faithful shall bear the invalidations and micro-aggressions of outrageous Patriarchy, they wilt really misplace their excrement when they get to that bit about 'God the Father.'

Hystericals 9:3

For only with the cooketh of yoke and the fryeth of swine shall thy sacred task complete.

Hashbrowns 7:17

✝

And so did spaghetti begat linguine, who begat fu silly, who begat tag lee a telly.

Pastas 4:3

And when Pharoh
commanded the changes, his
will was done with no
additional fee.

Clients 5:1

✝

An eye before eee less thy proceede sea.

Mnemonics 6:8

The Ford works in mysterious ways.

Mechanics 11:2

✝

Fear not! Salvation lies
beneath thy seat!

Flotations 1:1

Thou shall releaseth the
LORD, his followers,
brethren, and Disciples, from
and againsth any and all sin,
wars, plagues, causes of death,
fires, divorce, or incessant
desert wanderings arising
from or in connectioneth
with thy prayer, verse, or
psalm in accordance with the
word.

Indemnities 8:1

✝

Yea, hath ye cured my robes from stain and sweat, but mine cuff and pleat be far too rigid for my daily toil.

Cleaners 4:9

Whicheth of my brothers
heals thy skin and cureth thy
cancer? Yes.

Vitamins 3:12

✝

Then a third bell or peal of thunder. A man walked forth wearing glasses of no prescription. What rough beast is this, its hour come round at last, that slouches towards Brooklyn to be born?

Affectations 9:9

The foment lies within ye, lest ye unleash it.

Expulsions 18:2

✝

Grunts and whines and sullen silences will be thy only mode of speech. And the ground will be thy only haunt, for thou wilt be grounded. And thou wilt be known throughout the land as Insufferable, breaker of curfews.

Adolescents 16:1

And the lord sayeth; rest from your mallwalking and lean upon me for shall I not raise you up to the kingdom of retail?

Escalators 5:1

✝

Be strong and of a good courage, fear not of thine enemy for the Lord goes with thee; he will not fail thee, nor forsake thee. But just in case he doth be busy, stow thy Glock beneath thy robes.

Deuteronom-ish 31:6

For we brought nothing into this world, and we cannot take anything out of it if it be 3.5 fluid ounces or more

Transportations 12:1

✝

Thou shall maketh my mark upon the world, bigger.

Clients 10:17

Bless each meal with the sharing of an image, so that the multitude may feasteth their eyes, and liketh much.

Millennials 24:7

✝

Thou shall not freely offer hidden truths upon such times as thou have drinketh much.

Suggestions 12:3

Stars of Three. Thy work be great, yet thy kingdom haveth not abundant parking. And were art thou birthday cupcakes?

Reviews 10:2

✝

Though we have met at the light, let you not think that the slow way hath brought you here with me. The slowness of thine mechanical ass hath impeded my swiftness. A pox upon your house! A plague upon your land!

Drivers 15:35

So shall ye speak to the solicitors among ye so that they may say unto the robed host that which ye have related.

Affidavits 12:3

✝

Yay it is the 19 sheep nameth
Carl with cat glasses wears
upon him the baked bean
hats where upon the Lord
shall bring salvation sayeth
Leyroy the oldest of the Tree
Goats purple horse brick
spoons twenty two mommy

Mistranslations 4:67

Yea verily, I say unto thee if pleasure is brought to thee by it, then a ring of gold shouldst be bestowed upon it.

Beyonce 6:6

✝

The LORD did say unto me
when thou had left, 'Wow
that beith thy best joke thou
hath ever heard.' Then LORD
sayeth, 'thou must cometh to
heaven and bestow thy joke
for it will drench the
kingdom in thy giggly glory.'

Sarcasms 1:3

W U. GOD? B F F. O M G.
G.R 8 T.T.L

Acronyms 8:3

✝

Let he among you who is without sin throw the first stone, so that we might gang up on that self-righteous prick.

Blames 21:12

Knowest that thou art cursed
in my sight, and ev'ry tumbrel
or cart thou shalt take up in
the market place shall be
lame, and shalt stick on one
side, and make a terrible
noise, and thou wilt have to
use both hands to steer it, and
by this ye shall know my
displeasure with thee.

Grocers 5:7

✝

Clad in green and cuteness
shall they appear, offering the
thinnest of mints, temping
thou with gluttony.

Girlscouts 12:15

Vengeance is fine, sayeth the Lord.

Mistranslations 23:2

✝

Thou shall have no other dogs
before me.

Canines 6:24

SUBMIT YOUR OWN FAKE BIBLE VERSE

FAKEBIBLEVERSES.COM

To Graham, John, Terry, Eric, Michael, Terry and the Holy Hand Grenade of Antioch which they hath wrought; without which none of this would have been possible.

© 2021 Patrick E. McLean All Rights Reserved

While the authors and editor have made every attempt to present these amusements in the same spirit of divine playfulness that has inspired such creations as the platypus, the naked mole rat and the carrot top, we cannot be not responsible for any rift that the enjoyment of this work may cause with any denomination, synod, sect, cult, fraternal order, convention, Church, Facebook group or bowling club. Further, by reading this book you agree to hold the editor, publisher and authors harmless in the event of any divine judgement in the now or the hereafter.

Epigrammatic Press
An Awkward Division of Reinforcements, Inc.

Fake BIBLE ✝VERSES✝

Edited by
Patrick E. McLean

Written by
Patrick E. McLean, Adam Roe,
Brandon Scharr, Scott Helm

fakebibleverses.com

PRAISE FOR FAKE BIBLE QUOTES

"If you only read one entertainingly sacrilegious book this year, you are not welcome in our book club. Buy this book. Read it as an antidote to these dark times."
Erasmus Jones

"Five stars, five more stars, five million more stars, five billion trillion stars."
Hayden Planetarium

"I am pleased at thy good works in my name."
The Lord (thy God)

"Who am I to judge?"
Pope Francis

"Way funner than the Bible."
Bibliotheca Apostolica Vaticana

"Blessed are those who mourn, for they will be comforted. Blessed are the meek, for they will inherit the earth. And especially blessed are those who don't take things too seriously, because they're really going to love this book."
Matthew 5:3-6, Unauthorized Edition